DESERT DREAMS
OF
FAITH, HOPE, AND LOVE

DALE TWIGG

Copyright © 2024 by Dale Twigg

All rights reserved.

No portion of this book may be reproduced in any form without written permission from the publisher or author, except as permitted by U.S. copyright law.

For You Lord...

*Like a gentle wind
from so far away
I feel you
And in my desert dreams
I am wide awake
Stretching out my hands*

TABLE OF CONTENTS

FAITH 10

Let It Rain	12
Shower Eternal	14
Bring The Calm	15
Second Thoughts	16
Kaleidoscope	18
Icarus Sun	19
When I Arise	20
Take Me To The River	22
I'm Coming Home	24
The Divine Mystery	26
Www.blt	28
The Land Of Papier Mache'	29
Happy Birthday	31
Only Love	32
One More Day	34
Most High And Exalted	36
Antarctica	37
Forever More	38
Twilight	40
Into Your Arms Of Love	41
Joseph's Lullaby	42
I Am Home	43

HOPE 45

The Angels Cry For You	46
Crawl Inside	48
I'll Carry You	49
Farmer's Lament	52
The Sun Will Come Up	54
I'll Be There	56
Seeds	58
I Am The Light	60
It's In The Walk	61
I'll Take You Away	63
We Will Fly	65
All By Myself	67
Winking At Me	68
Autumn	70
In The Sweetest Stillness	71
Free To Be	73
God Of Israel	75
The Last Tear	77

LOVE 79

On The Edge	80
Daydream	81
One Sultry Night	82
Don't Speak	83
All Day Long	84
Speak To Me	86
My Blessed Valentine	87
Like...	89
My Living Dream	90
Oh That I….	92
The Poem Within The Poem	93
The Opal Orchid	94
I Am There	95
Speaking Only With Our Eyes	97
Kisses	99
As The Fireflies Dance	101
Hidden Treasure	102
You Are My...	104
About The Author	106

FAITH

Faith

*There is no grander sword
dare the bravest knight afford
to rend the hearts of men
than the humble poet's pen*

LET IT RAIN

It's been forty long days,
And I'm tired of this wasteland
Lord please show me Your ways,
Bring me back to Your Graceland

My soul is cracked and dry,
Lord please open up the sky
And let it rain

Rain, Rain on me now,
Won't You pour, Pour Your love down
Let Your love flow on down, And soak me to the ground
And let it rain

It's been forty long nights,
And I'm tired of the nightmares
Lord please help me in this fight,
I know you will help me get there

When I'm weak, you are strong,
But Lord please don't take too long
Let it rain

Faith

Rain, Rain on me now,
Won't You pour, Pour Your love down
Let Your love flow on down, And soak me to the ground
And let it rain

I know You will find a way,
And there will be better days
Lord let Your love shine through,
Because I trust in You

So let it rain....

SHOWER ETERNAL

Trickle, trickle,
the rain does trickle,
clear and fresh
it seeps into my soul
like butter on a hot bun

My mind,
a sponge of confusion,
unrest, and turbulence,
soaking up the gift of life
to quench my dry bedlam

This shower eternal,
it cleanses my soul,
wipes my worldly blemishes,
filtering my tap water veins
into purity and peace

Drenched in light,
and overwhelming love,
I stand in the Heavenly dew,
lifting my feathery arms
to the One behind it all

Faith

BRING THE CALM

Oh how my mind heaves to and fro
As the pitch and roll of the boat moves so

With each crashing wave that threatens
My heart all the more it beckons

Speak to me with tender song
For only your voice can bring the calm

To soften the sea of my stormy soul
And make me now eternally whole

SECOND THOUGHTS

The wheels are turning,
cogs are churning,
it's a black hole mystery
Flowers are popping,
life is stopping,
what is the world to be?

Walking, walking,
always walking,
with head on heal and toe
Talking, talking,
always talking,
no thoughts of where to go

Slow down,
don't drown,
stop time for just a glance
Look around,
hear the sound,
second thoughts give the chance

Faith

To look and see,
and to be free,
think not of this old world
But upon a tree
He died for me,
and true life will be unfurled

KALEIDOSCOPE

I am a kaleidoscope
swirling around the bed
of someone else's dreams

And oh what pretty colors
that I can produce
for someone else's eyes

But to what extent
do I twist myself
for someone else's joy?

I need colors of my own
to sift and to sway
and light my own dreams

Faith

ICARUS SUN

O Come, O come, Icarus Sun,
Melt these wings that I have on.

Far too long I have worn them wrong,
Where one-way dreams do belong.

So much to fight both tooth and nail,
Only to build for myself a jail.

Freedom is found not in flying away,
But in knowing you can…..

And choosing to stay.

WHEN I ARISE

When I arise and see your face,
it reflects the sun's warm embrace,
dispels the gloom of last night's rain
and takes away my secret pain

that pain that haunts my dreams sometimes
and drowns out the church bell chimes.
Too many times, too many times
it has drowned out the church bell chimes.

But not anymore......

When I arise and see your face,
it reflects the sun's warm embrace,
dispels the gloom of last night's rain
and takes away my secret pain.

Faith

*You can never live
without fear and failure;
they are a part
of enliving your dream.
Embrace them
and you will find
that failure becomes your tutor
to try again,
and fear becomes your catalyst
to never give up.*

TAKE ME TO THE RIVER

My life before wasn't something to be proud of
It was filled with dirty stains
But then You came and over-flooded my soul
And You washed me clean

So I said to You, Oh I said to You.....

Take me to the river, take me down, take me down
Take me to the river, take me down, on Holy Ground
Take me to the river, take me down, take me down
Take me to the river, take me down, new life is found

Now I stand on the banks of this precious water
Asking You to cleanse my soul
Take my life and all of the broken pieces
Lord please make me whole

Faith

And I say to You, Yes I say to You.....

Take me to the river, take me down, take me down
Take me to the river, take me down, on Holy Ground
Take me to the river, take me down, take me down
Take me to the river, take me down, new life is found

Desert Dreams

I'M COMING HOME

Traveling down along this rainy road
with my face into the wind,
I need a place to lay this heavy load
and someone to take me in.

You are there with your arms open wide
in a place where I belong;
the more I search, the more I come to find
the place was there all along.

I'm coming home, I'm coming home
And I'll never ever have to be alone
I've finally found a place where I call home

They say that home is where the heart is,
and I'm inclined to agree;
I have found a special peace within
Because You have set me free.

Faith

I'm coming home, I'm coming home
And I'll never ever have to be alone
I've finally found a place where I call home

High up in the sky where eagles fly,
That is where I call home.
I will spread my wings as angels sing,
Praise the Lord, I'm coming home.

I'm coming home, I'm coming home
And I'll never ever have to be alone
I've finally found a place where I call home

THE DIVINE MYSTERY

Lord you are a divine mystery
How can I gaze into the eyes of Thee?
So transcendent and so holy,
Yet Your touch melts the heart of me.

Behold the Divine Mystery,
So much more than we can see.
Embrace the Divine Mystery,
A precious wonder is He.

Golden treasures, silver and pearls,
A mere hand-breath of this finite world.
Mighty princes, wise me of old,
Could not reveal Your ways unfurled.

Behold the Divine Mystery,
So much more than we can see.
Embrace the Divine Mystery,
A precious wonder is He.

Faith

You came out of Your eternity,
To heal the lame, make the blind see.
Above all rule and authority,
You bless the humble and lift the lowly.

Behold the Divine Mystery,
So much more than we can see.
Embrace the Divine Mystery,
A precious wonder is He.

WWW.BLT

(The wide wonderful world of BIG little things)

It often takes the precious mind of a child, and its profound ability to make the small and insignificant things in this world seem larger than life.....

To show us the wondrous difference between merely catching a firefly, and owning a kingdom in a jar.

Faith

THE LAND OF PAPIER MACHE'

In the Land of Papier Mache'
are children not of this world,
living life day by day
with eternity unfurled.

A land of unending dreams
where abstract words are real,
and have become tangible
to see and smell and feel.

A land of words, you know them:
love and happiness,
that are not words but people
to hug and hold and kiss.

A land where people age
from death to life again,
where women are treated like queens
by true noble gentlemen.

Desert Dreams

A land of candy with streams of milk
and fields of peppermint,
and Christmas trees all year 'round
and sunsets of every tint.

A land where adults are infants
who ride on giant frogs,
where the sun is the lord of the day,
and his soldiers are puppy dogs.

A land of love so real and alive
that you can hug and hold all day,
and keep it as your very own
in the Land of Papier Mache'.

Faith

HAPPY BIRTHDAY

I never imagined the sun
could change its path
but today it did
for you

I watched as it seemed
to follow me,
painting expressions
of indigo and gold

And I wondered why it was
that the sun
was so kind to change
for just one

Then I realized, years ago,
God made you for this day
and today, as a gift,
He is making this day
for me

ONLY LOVE

Lord, I did it again,
I stepped out in sin
I'm so tired of what I do,
And I'm sure You're tired too

But just when I think,
That I'm about to sink
You reach out Your hand,
And lift me out of the sand

Love, only love
Love, only love
That's what You have for me
Love, only love

Lord, I'm still walking around,
with my head hanging down
You shed Your blood to set me free,
And put Your Spirit inside me

Faith

So I step out in faith,
And cast off this weight
And reach out my hand,
And grab hold Your plan

Love, only love
Love, only love
That's what I have for You
Love, only love

Desert Dreams

ONE MORE DAY

A thousand thunderous hoof beats
pounding down upon my chest,
Could not arrest my heart that beats
the passion within my breast

A hearkened plea to draw you near
amidst the sweeping swirling fray,
And gaze your eyes so lovely dear
to have you just for one more day

I'd cross a hundred million miles
through ocean currents thick with foam,
Face frigid frost and fiery trials
and make loneliness my home

I'd declare to all the world
in peerless fashion and display,
My pledge to you fully unfurled
to have you just for one more day

Faith

Countless armies rising high
marching on against my back,
Cannot quell the joyous cry
of victory when I attack

With all the strength within my heart
I'll fight on to make a way,
Til even 'death do us part'
to have you just for one more day

I say chivalry is alive
it's living strong within my soul,
Trust and honor is the drive
your tender heart is the goal

So do not doubt, my precious love
I'm coming to you without delay,
And bringing Heaven from above
to have you just for one more day

MOST HIGH AND EXALTED

You know my heart, Lord,
and when I'm weak
But Your steadfast love,
it will never cease

And Your mercy, Lord,
it will never end
And at the dawn,
comes Your faithfulness again

Praise You Lord,
I will praise You Lord;
Praise You Lord,
You are God Most High and Exalted

Faith

ANTARCTICA

Like a sea of a thousand crystals
tiny prisms of the sun
the thick layers of ice crackle
with each footfall in the virgin snow

The winds muse their song
in harmony with the brush-stroked sky
a symphony of keyless chords
heard only by the angels, until now

Tall I stand in this vast expanse
as I gaze in spectral wonder
at the bitterness and beauty
of the absence of nature

And I bravely breathe aloud
like billowing clouds of smoke
a song that signals life
at the top of the bottom of the world

FOREVER MORE

Praise you Lord, You're my Savior
My King of Kings
Praise You Lord, You're my Savior
My Lord of Lords
Praise You Lord, You're my Savior
I'll worship You this day,
And Forever more

Praise You Lord, You're my Healer
Come heal my soul
Praise You Lord, You're my Healer
Come make me whole
Praise You Lord, You're my Healer
I'll worship You this day,
And Forever more

Faith

Praise You Lord, my Provider
My Bread of Life
Praise You Lord, my Provider
I'm free from strife
Praise You Lord, my Provider
I'll worship You this day,
And Forever more

Praise You Lord, my Redeemer
My soul will sing
Praise You Lord, my Redeemer
My everything
Praise You Lord, my Redeemer
I'll worship You this day,
And Forever more

TWILIGHT

The sun has just set,
yet evidence of it lingers
on the near edge of the horizon,
in a glow of salmon and gold.

Shadows steal away
to embrace the eager evening,
as the day's clamor is swallowed
by a slow and slinking hush.

Warmly one by one,
little lazy lights appear
in dim and distant windows,
as children settle in for sleep.

All is quiet now,
to hear one's breath and beating heart
in the peace and silent solace
of the taming of the night

Faith

INTO YOUR ARMS OF LOVE

My Lord, my King, I hear the hoof-beats comin'

My Lord, I sing, with all the angels strummin'

Take me home , Into Your arms of love

My Lord, my Friend,
I see Your arms out-stretchin'

My Lord, please send, Your Spirit soon a-fetchin'

Take me home, Into Your arms of love

Into Your arms of love

JOSEPH'S LULLABY

Oh Baby Jesus, asleep in the straw,
I can't believe you are the Son of God.
Those precious hands and those feet are so small;
Who would ever think you are Lord of all.

But I heard the angels sing, announcing your birth:
'The Savior of the world has come to earth!'
The prophets have foretold of this, the chosen seed,
and the day will come when those hands and feet will bleed.

One great price to pay to end all my strife;
Clinging to a tree to give me your life.

Oh Baby Jesus, asleep in the straw,
I do believe you are the Son of God.
Rest your head now in my arms you will stay,
and I will worship you, my King, this day.

I AM HOME

Sometimes at night, when I am all alone
And I have no where to go,
I cry to You, and You see me through,
You tell me I am not alone

In Your arms Lord, I am home
There is no other place I'd rather be,
Cuz in Your arms Lord, I am home
I am home

Sometimes this life, is so hard to live
But I will live it for You,
Cuz in the end, I know that I will spend
All eternity with You

In Your arms Lord, I am home
There is no other place I'd rather be,
Cuz in Your arms Lord, I am home
I am home

Lord it seems I've been waiting so long
For my time to come
But with You all the waiting is gone,
And I know where I belong

In Your arms Lord, I am home
There is no other place I'd rather be,
Cuz in Your arms Lord, I am home
I am home

HOPE

THE ANGELS CRY FOR YOU

It's a long way downtown
in the pouring rain
Did you take enough money
to find your way?

You say Momma won't listen,
Daddy doesn't care
But is the answer really to
run away from there?

I know you are hurting,
I see your pain
But will you take the time to listen,
listen to the rain?

Cause I hear up in Heaven,
they know your name
And they share all your sorrows
every time it rains

Hope

Don't run away, child,
if you only knew
Don't you know, child,
the angels cry for you

Just how do you plan to make it,
living on the streets?
And now will you sell yourself
to the ones you meet?

Don't you know you are precious,
precious all the time,
To the One who made you
beautifully divine

Don't run away, child,
if you only knew
Don't you know, child,
the angels cry for you

It's a long way downtown
in the pouring rain
Won't you come take my hand,
I'll show you the way

You have so much to give,
your heart is strong
Just believe in your dreams,
all you need is one

CRAWL INSIDE

*Who will wonder, and who will care
of those things I ponder, those dreams I dare,
those monsters I battle, those songs I sing
in the silence of my mind that moonlight brings?*

*The eyes of my heart are open wide-
will you look and listen......and crawl inside?*

Hope

I'LL CARRY YOU

I hear your voice, in the silence of the snow,
as you call out to me
You're making angels, in a devil's world,
and all you want to be is free

And I know that sometimes, you just want to
quit,
I have felt that way too
But there's just one thing, that you have to know
to help see you through

When you're walking through the storm,
and your feet are tired and worn....

I'll carry you, when you feel you can't go on
I'll carry you, when you believe that you were
wrong
I'll carry you

I see your face, as bright as the sun,
as you look up at me
You're trying so hard, just to be loved,
When all you have to do is be

Desert Dreams

And I know that sometimes, you just want to quit,
I have felt that way too
But there's just one thing, that you have to know to help see you through

When you're trying hard to find,
that love to ease your mind...

I'll carry you, when no one will understand,
I'll carry you, when you need to hold a hand,
I'll carry you

I know you're waiting, waiting for that day,
that final moment, when you lay your burdens down
And in the coming, the coming of that day,
rest assured my love, that I will be around...

I'll carry you, through the open door
I'll carry you, and we'll live forever more
I'll carry you

*Through happiness
we experience
the sheer wonder
of life*

*And through heartache
we discover
its immeasurable
worth*

FARMER'S LAMENT

Behold her tearful April face
Sweet September's soft embrace
Is cracked and dry from Winter's chill
Dead February stiff and still

O how the seasons take their toll
To rapture such a youthful soul

Childish treasures the robin brings
Back in the Spring of dreamy things
Have fallen like a seed unsown
A hallowed hemlock's silent grown

Strip asunder O plowman's blade
Every shoot of grass and glade
To catch the harvest of early year
The Reaper's grim appointment dear

Winter waters raging edge
Prefer the snow to sleet instead
To receive the better pure
Nature's way the fine to lure

Hope

Misery burns under the sun
To flame the Summer heat of pain
But in this fire there stands One
Who soothes the heat with cooling rain

Death drags on in calendar rows
To soon release its morbid pose
For orchids blossom life again
But must this child wait 'til then?

O how the seasons take their toll
To rapture such a youthful soul

THE SUN WILL COME UP

Wintery winds wisp along like tails
Whipping at my face and making trails
All along my mind as I think of you
And the wretched pain that you went through.

I understand as I sit here in the snow
Ready to lay myself down, down below,
And stretch out my arms, and my legs too
To make a crystalline angel, just for you.

One that cries when you cry,
weeps when you weep
Laughs when you laugh,
and sleeps when you sleep,
Forgets when you want,
remembers when you won't,
Loves when you need it,
and stays close when you don't.

Hope

Those wintery winds don't have to be so cold
If there are warm hands around your
heart to hold;
Come inside where there is safety glowing bright
And peaceful gentle arms to wrap
around you tight.

I will hold you if you let me, so don't be afraid
There are plenty of tomorrows still to be made;
The sun will come up, and so will your soul,
and there you will dance beautifully whole.

I'LL BE THERE

You've been waiting too long,
And now you're just hanging on
You need a place to find that peace of mind
where all your cares are gone

Won't you come take my hand,
I will help you to stand
I will be the one, the only one
who can pull you from the sand

I'll be there, in the pouring rain,
and your deepest pain
I'll be there, in your saddest song,
and things go wrong
I'll be there, in your darkest days,
and all your ways
I'll be there, I'll be there

Hope

I can see it in your eyes
A new day that will rise
I will be the one, the only one
to lift you up through the skies

I'll be there, in the shining sun,
and all you've done
I'll be there, on your highest hill,
your greatest thrill
I'll be there, in your brightest days,
and all your ways
I'll be there, I'll be there

I will never leave you,
or forsake you
I'll be there, I'll be there
for you

SEEDS

I can hear it when we speak,
those whispers between words
of thoughts that form
but have yet to be spoken;

Thoughts of distant stars
yet to be born;
now just small seeds
harbored within your soul.

I have them too,
deep inside my being,
echoing the silent sentences
that only romance can own.

Those fears that creep upon you
in the twilight of night,
those monsters of the mind
you so desperately avoid,

Hope

I will protect you from,
battle against,
even bleed myself out,
to water those seeds

.....with hope;

Hope that there truly is one
with whom you can be safe,
and be the little girl
you never knew.

Let me hold you tonight
and carry you away,
away with the winds
on a world without maps,

Until we reach that sacred space
between earth and heaven,
when the morning gathers us
to a star all our own.....

I AM THE LIGHT

Somewhere someone whispers
Somewhere someone shivers
Every footfall
I hear it all
I am the night

Someone lights a candle
Someone can barely handle
I'll take your heart
All broken apart
I am the night

Somehow time is slowing
Somehow flowers are growing
Gone is the night
Won is the fight
I am the Light

Hope

IT'S IN THE WALK

The sun is ablaze and fiery bronze
as it sips the salty sea.
Wearing a golden crown of clouds
and stars of dazzling diadems,
it sits upon its watery throne.

There you stand, watching and waiting,
for that speck of hope on the horizon,
hope for that verdant vessel bearing
all your weekly waltzing wishes,
and your daily dancing dreams.

But your cheeks grow warm and wet,
and the seagulls cry with you,
as you candidly come to find
that the only thing that arrives
is the twinkling tide of twilight.

Then, like a hurricane of rain,
It pelts you and you fall,
knees in the sand, toes in the foam,
and I am there, to grasp your hand,
meet your gaze, and harbor you.

Desert Dreams

And in that singular sullen moment,
you realize your ship has already come-
in the heartbeat of an embrace,
and the warmth of a whisper
that softly says 'its gonna be alright'.

So tread with me now along the beach,
however far its sandy shore may go.
For it's not in the wind and waves you seek,
it's in the walk, with hand in hand,
where your longing will find a home.

Hope

I'LL TAKE YOU AWAY

I went and bought a boat today;
It was rusty, old, and gray (but I knew)
Time would help me find a way
To lift its sail and take me away.

You were staring at the shore,
Just like the day before (and I saw)
Tears roll down and hit the floor;
You were dreaming of a place
Where tears upon your face were no more.

There's a boat leaving today
And it's coming your way,
Just climb aboard, and I'll take you away.
We will search the open sea
For a place to be free;
Just take my hand, and I'll take you away
with me.

We've been through some hard times,
And many things that didn't rhyme (but I think)
I can read between the lines;
Your pain this time is harder than mine.

Desert Dreams

I want to take it all away,
Without fear or delay (but I know)
Time will somehow make a way;
And until that time comes,
I'll give you all the love I can today.

There's a boat leaving today
And it's coming your way,
Just climb aboard, and I'll take you away.
We will search the open sea
For a place to be free;
Just take my hand, and I'll take you away
with me.

We will paint our dreams on canvas
And hoist them high into the blue;
And let the wind gently sail us,
Until all our dreams come true.

Hope

WE WILL FLY

One lazy Sunday, I saw you on the porch
You were staring at the sky
It seemed as though that day was the worst
You and me, we held and cried

You were looking for a day to be free
Graceful mountains to climb
Now you're older and it's me, don't you see
Your day of freedom has arrived

I am yours, you are mine
And together we will fly
I am yours, you are mine
And together, we will fly

You see my child, there's no room to fear
Just take your wings and fly
There is no greater love than this
Than for a friend, to die

Desert Dreams

Please don't let the world pass you by
You have so much to give
I'll be here, right by your side
So come with me, and live

I am yours, you are mine
And together we will fly
I am yours, you are mine
and together, we will fly

Hope

ALL BY MYSELF

There is no greater desire that I have in life
than to find a small seed, born out of strife,

and plant it in the soil of my secret garden
that I myself know will never harden;

I will sweat and toil and even bleed
to carefully crack open that helpless seed

and nourish the growth of that dear precious find
with the warmth of my heart and the
strength of my mind,

ever so gently pruning the leaves that are torn
to make lots of room for new ones to be born,

until that blessed moment when the blossom arrives,
far too beautiful for the rest of the worlds eyes,

that I have to take it home, make room on my shelf
and forever adore it, all by myself.

WINKING AT ME

The brash of the day is on simmer
As the shadows flee from the sun,
In the twilight stars start to glimmer
as they each greet me one by one.

And as I stare at them they stare back
As if seeing just what I can see,
And I can't help but accept the fact
They are winking, winking at me.

Could it be God has heard my cry
As I call in the middle of night,
My dreams and my beckoning sigh
As I pray with all of my might.

All those hopes I have tucked away
In a place only He and I know,
That I take out on a rainy day
To fight the fears I battle so.

Hope

Could it be He is answering now
All my dreams and hopes and sighs,
As I watch the heavens bow
In these silent twinkling skies.

With sweaty palms and a misty stare
I am struck at what I see,
You standing radiantly there
And you are winking, winking at me.

AUTUMN

The air is crisp and clean
like a glassy sheen
of mist and myrrh

Pumpkins sing their trilly tune
while children play at noon
in leaves of gold

Happy are the apple trees
and the Autumn breeze
cool on my face

Sunsets throw a lovely glow
red and yellow colors flow
until the night beckons

This is the subtle season
for no rhyme or reason
just peace and joy

Hope

IN THE SWEETEST STILLNESS

A host of angels stand, eyes a wide
As God Eternal sets time aside,
Steps into the skin of mortal man,
And not just man, but a little lamb.

A lamb of sacrifice for all mankind
Willing to leave none behind,
If only they would look up and see
And follow the star to a wee baby.

The angels knew, the shepherds too
That love was born, and reborn anew,
In the sweetest stillness of the night
New creation came, our Eternal Light.

God's master stroke of grace and love
Sent to we mere mortals from above,
None deserved, and yet none denied,
Born for us to be crucified.

This silent night, this special night
The angels welcome the Eternal Light,
This tiny babe so meek and small
Will grow to one day save us all.

Hope

FREE TO BE

I saw a man crying in the rain today
His eyes met mine but he had no words to say
It pierced my soul to see him suffer so,
Now I know, yes I know...

Standing in the rain, I looked deep in my heart
Into my emptiness and wanderings in the dark
And how I hide my pain to put on a show,
Now I know, yes I know...

It was Jesus, hanging on a cross
It was Jesus, saving the lost
It was Jesus, touching me
Now I'm free, free to be me

The me I choose to be lives for Him today
I lay down my crown as He comes my way
And we shall celebrate the joy of Heaven so,
Now I know, yes I know...

Desert Dreams

I know that He has risen in glory today
I feel my sins forgiven in a powerful way
I gaze His beauty and watch His glory grow,
Now I know, yes I know...

It is Jesus, reigning on the throne
It is Jesus, calling me home
It is Jesus, revealing this,
I am free, free to be His

GOD OF ISRAEL

The oceans roar, the fields adore
Your mighty hand that makes rivers tame
You opened the sea, set Your people free
And crushed all enemies that profaned Your name

Hallelujah, Hallelujah
Baruch Adonai, Elohe Yisrael
Hallelujah, Hallelujah
Blessed be the Lord, God of Israel

David our King, taught us to sing
Seek Your beauty, dance before Your throne
Your name we praise, Oh Ancient of Days
Messiah come, come to claim Your own

Hallelujah, Hallelujah
Baruch Adonai, Elohe Yisrael
Hallelujah, Hallelujah
Blessed be the Lord, God of Israel

You sent Your Son, Your chosen One
Spotless from Heaven, a sacrificial lamb
Jesus our King, salvation bring
We worship You, our great I Am

Hallelujah, Hallelujah
Baruch Adonai, Elohe Yisrael
Hallelujah, Hallelujah
Blessed be the Lord, God of Israel

THE LAST TEAR

There have been days
yes I know them well
where I cried me a river
and watched it swell

Into a torrent
of pain and regret
that would not dare
ever let me forget

But the older I grow
the more that I know
that those rivers of pain
will soon turn to snow

And melt in the sun
of the coming Spring
and the warmth of the love
that only You can bring

Desert Dreams

Until that final day
where You show me the jar
of all the drops You collected
both near and so far

Of the pain I endured
and cried deep and wide
trying so desperately
from others to hide

And with one gentle stroke
You will lift up my head
and wipe forever away
the last tear I will shed

LOVE

ON THE EDGE

Far away from busy banquet halls,
somewhere near misty waterfalls,
there is a place you can call your own
that cannot be reached by telephone;
a magical place, on the edge of romance,
known only by those who took the chance
to live,
to laugh,
to love.

I am there, will you join me tonight,
for a picnic, by candlelight?
With chocolates and strawberries and
pink champagne,
and music so sweet... it will drive you insane.
But, alas, until then, I will leave you with this:
a soft caress,
and one,
gentle
kiss.

Love

DAYDREAM

From across the room
I stared at you,
and the skin on my arms
tingled
as I thought of a better place
where you and I were free....
free to be ourselves
and speak without words.

Like a silly schoolboy
I tried to avoid your eyes
but you captured me
and I fell into them
like a slow moving river,
cool and gentle.

God, I wanted to stay there,
long into the night,
just floating in your eyes;
but the sun was going to sleep
and my daydream was,
as all daydreams are....
only good for the day.

Desert Dreams

ONE SULTRY NIGHT

One sultry night where angels rule,
the moon was bright, hung like a jewel
around your neck and descending down
across your skin so softly brown.

Dare I breathe and steal away
the one sweet chance to hear you say,
within your sleep and gentle dreams,
your love for me is as it seems?

A thousand breaths, a million sighs,
I'd gladly trade to realize
that moment of truth and treasure alike
for which princes prize and warriors fight

To own the space within the heart
of one so fair as you. Depart,
depart my fears, just for tonight-
this moment's mine 'til morning light.

Love

DON'T SPEAK

Will you let the wind
carry my voice
to the ear of your heart?

Can I sing a song
of romance
composed for your eyes?

Will you watch and listen
as I speak
without a word?

Can you hear me?
shhh.....darling,
don't speak.

ALL DAY LONG

All day long I saw your pretty green eyes
staring at me

through the budding trees and grassy shoots
of newborn Spring

The pitch and timbre of soft tones
collided

at just the right moment to create
the most beautiful sound:

pure silence wherewith I could hear
the wind

carry your name, not to my ear,
but to my heart

Where I chose to wear it from the moment your
soft lips

touched mine in a twilight embrace
that lingers still

*Eyes truly are the windows of the soul.
No sound is needed to hear two lovers whisper.
Just look into their eyes,
in the candlelight of their dreams.*

*You will hear the pounding thunder,
the thunder of their hearts.
Beating in pure silence,
and making pure magic.*

SPEAK TO ME

There is no greater feeling
than the touch of your lips,
pressing gently upon mine

It is like sleeping
in sheets of crushed velvet,
bathing in crimson wine

Do you feel the soft petals,
smell the sweet fragrance
of what is in my mind?

Can you speak the language
of unspoken words?
Speak to me, divine

Love

MY BLESSED VALENTINE

Sometimes at night I think of you and me
sitting alone under a tree
in the Garden of Eden.

And that special day that created the joy
of the magic innocence of a girl and boy,
so playfully in love.

You and I under the tree,
unashamed of what we see;
so beautiful and free.

The tropical breeze becomes a test
of the heated passion in my chest
for one so lovely as you.

Oh be my blessed Valentine
with celebrated gifts of wine
to capture the youth of my soul.

Desert Dreams

And I will give you all the world,
or maybe, just my heart unfurled;
filled with nothing but the fragrance
of you.

Love

LIKE...

...ripples on a pond,

Your touch abruptly stirs
the still waters of my heart

Yet calms the raging sea
within my troubled mind

And floods the very depths
of the streams of my soul.

...a solitary rose,

You catch my passing by
and slowly slow me down

To breathe in your beauty
and smell your every scent

And bask in the wonder
of you becoming my dream

Desert Dreams

MY LIVING DREAM

Girl, you are, oh so beautiful to me
When you stand in the mirror, I wish you could see
Girl, you have such a lovely spirit, you do
And it shines so brightly, like the sun coming through

You will see just how bright,
And I'll show you, tonight....

I'll dress you up, and take you out
Help you see, you are to me
My living dream

Girl, with you, there is no one else on the earth
And I'll spend my whole life, just to show you your worth
Girl, I am here, so come, take my hand
And I'll give you my heart, and together we'll stand

Love

Our future looks so bright
And it's starting, tonight....

I'll dress you up, and take you out
Help you see, you are to me
My living dream

When I kiss you, I will kiss you, and hold you tight
When I love you, I will love you, all through the night

I'll dress you up, and take you out
Help you see, you are to me
My living dream

OH THAT I....

could hush the hands of time,
for only but a moment;
to preserve a precious place,
a small sacred spot,
on Eternity's timeless chain.

To capture forever,
the wonder witnessed now;
the miraculous birth
of two hearts joining as one,
by the gentle hands of God.

There is no other place
that I would rather be,
than in this singular moment,
alone here with you;
but look around, my Love....

We have an audience of angels.

THE POEM WITHIN THE POEM

Your face is like a poem, my darling, my bride,
with well thought-out couplets arranged side by side,
that flow with a rhythm so effortless and free,
revealing a master poet's true mastery.

And as I dare gaze in your soft lovely eyes,
I fall quite headlong between the fine lines,
and find there the message, a sweet song of truth,
composed by the poet; a masterful muse.

A sweet song of hope the poet joyfully sings,
to fit this earthen angel with trapezious wings,
and soar to the rescue of weary-worn souls,
that I find myself to be one, behold.

How humble and gracious, a commoner such as I,
should be so duly chosen by the poet to confide,
not just the writing on this fair face all can see,
but the poem within the poem, written so

beautifully for me.

THE OPAL ORCHID

What looming dust from the edge of time
Does mortal men bring down from here

Where dew drips like honey from the rim
Of fresh flowers bigger than stars thrown
Across the universe and yet tender than
The smallest stamen in an opal orchid

I hear the cries of the sweet sirens song
As they sing silently for me and for you

Waiting and watching while the wind plays
The grass laughs and the sidewalk smiles
Together to bring loneliness to an end
Where there once was only crowded emptiness

Now you and I can play with the opal orchid
And then drink the dew of joyfulness

Hiding time like a buried treasure and
Waiting only for our hearts to sync in rhyme
With the crashing of the distant waves
And the setting sun glistening beneath our feet

Love

I AM THERE

I am there
where the ocean meets the air,
in the misty molecules
you'll find my follicles
of hair in your hand
as we rest upon the sand.

We lay there as one
under the warm setting sun
to freely glance
the glorious romance
of God's divine bliss
as our silhouettes kiss.

As the harbor lights dim
past the moon's glowing rim
all I can see
are your eyes playfully
dancing along
with my heart's beating song.

Desert Dreams

And my very soul is spent
to purchase the scent
of your skin on mine,
forever entwined
in this divine embrace
too intricate to trace.

Love

SPEAKING ONLY WITH OUR EYES

You came across my mind today
and don't you know, I had no words to say
It's getting harder now to speak
there's something greater that I wish to seek

I want to hear the whispers of your heart
screaming oh so loud and clear...

I am waiting for that blessed day
the day your heart and soul entwine with mine
And I know upon that blessed day
we will sail though each other's minds
speaking only with our eyes

There's so much that I want to say
but sometimes words just get in the way
It's something that we both must feel
to make the love between us more than real

Do you hear the whispers of my heart
screaming oh so loud and clear...

Desert Dreams

Are you waiting for that blessed day
the day my heart and soul entwine with yours
Do you know upon that blessed day
we will sail through each other's minds
speaking only with our eyes

You came across my mind today
and you heard every word that I had to say
It's getting easy now to speak
because your lovely eyes are all I seek

KISSES

The angels are crying now;
I can feel them on my face
as I look up and search
for your reflection in the moon.

The moon, like a quiet glowing orb,
becomes anything I want
if I pray hard enough
and cry large tears.

Tears are the wellspring
that feeds my soul,
a never-ending hunger
for something eternal.

Eternal desires dug deep down
in my morass of thoughts,
too lofty for words.....
but not for kisses.

Kisses of laughter
long echoed from your lips,
heard now with the angels
and the smile of the moon.

AS THE FIREFLIES DANCE

Like the sweet smell of honeysuckle in the late
hours of Spring,
The fragrance of your soft skin lingers on the
empty linen.

I stretch out my hand to the gentle wind that
whispers warm,
Like the very breath of God, and send a kiss to
your tender lips.

Come, let us unite our gaze toward the same
somber moon,
As the fireflies dance to the silent tune of our
beating hearts.

Far away but ever close, we embrace again for but
a moment,
And drink deep the sullied sweetness of a
treasured memory.

HIDDEN TREASURE

When diamonds turn to dust,
and flowers slowly fade
Silver soon will rust, and friends go their way
I know there's something better
I've been longing for

Been trying my whole life, to fill my empty heart
Through struggle, pain, and strife, I found the missing part
It's a hidden treasure, I buried long before

All those dark and wasted years
Of chasing dreams and gaining tears,
I should have noticed from the start,
The hidden treasure in my heart

The colors from my past,
that once were black and gray
Have now faded fast, and become bright as day
And I've learned to measure things
worth fighting for

Love

I lift my voice up loud and cry
to the angels in the sky,
And proclaim to the world,

Something beautiful, that I always knew;
My hidden treasure....
is You

YOU ARE MY...

Oh Lord how beautiful, in this quiet room
is Your presence with me, I bow to You.
You have saved my life from sore distress,
and now I give it to You; I enter Your rest.

You are my... Great Redeemer
You are my... Savior
You are my... Precious Spirit
You are my... Holy Lord
You are my... King

Before I close my eyes, I sing to You,
a thankful song of praise for all You do.
But as I gaze at You. I'm struck by what I see;
beyond all that You do, it's who You are to me.

You are my... Eternal Father
You are my... Prince of Peace
You are my... Closest Brother
You are my... Sweet Release
You are my... Friend

Love

Oh Lord, you and me, we have seen so much,
and now my soul is yearning; I need Your touch.
So many ups and downs that I have been through,
have brought a peace that helps me truly know
You.

You are my... Hallelujah
You are my... Praise the Lord
You are my... Glory Jesus
You are my... Living Word
You are my... Love

About the Author

Rev. Dale Twigg, MDiv. has spent his whole life around literature and music. His favorite book being the Bible. Dale grew up in Pittsburgh, PA and felt a tug on his heart from the Lord at an early age. He has been writing poems and songs ever since to reflect his faith in the one true Lover of his soul. He is a graduate of Westminster Theological Seminary near Philadelphia, PA where he works as a Hospice Chaplain to comfort the dying, and as a Missionary to aid the poor and needy around the world.

Made in United States
Cleveland, OH
19 January 2025